Overcoming Obstacles: Being All That God Created You to Be

Acknowledgements

I would like to thank my late mother for raising me to be the young man that I am today. I would also like to thank my wife for always supporting me in my endeavors. I would also like to thank my father-in-law for always being there for me and supporting me in my quest to make this book a reality.

Contents

1. Acknowledgements
2. Introduction
3. Humble Beginnings
4. Timing Is Everything
5. When Life Knocks You Down, Seek God
6. Forgiving Those Who Betray You
7. Pressing Forward In Spite of Criticism
8. Being Content In Every Situation
9. Trusting God
10. It's Really Not About You
11. Walking In Your Destiny
12. Using What God Has Gifted You With
13. Get Ready For Your Comeback
14. God Is Always There
15. Don't Fold Under Pressure
16. Sharing The Load
17. Overcoming Obstacles

Introduction

I have overcome a lot of obstacles in my life, but if I had to choose a period of adversity in my life that was the most difficult to overcome, then it would have to be the death of my mother. It happened my senior year of high school, just as I was preparing to graduate and go off to college. This should have been one of the happiest times in my life, but instead of being filled with great joy, I was stricken with grief. Honestly, I wasn't prepared to lose her and in addition to my Father in heaven, she was everything to me.

How do you overcome losing something or someone that was extremely important to you? How do you continue to carry on that person's legacy now that they are no longer here? How do you move forward after the death of a loved one? The answer was a simple one for me. I decided to trust God to get me through the tough times. Isaiah 26:3 NIV says, "You will keep in perfect peace those whose minds are steadfast, because they trust in you." The Amplified Bible says, "You will guard him and keep him in perfect and constant peace whose mind [both its inclination and its character] is stayed on you, because he commits himself to you, leans on you, and hopes confidently in you." During those tough times, Isaiah 26:3 became the scripture upon which I leaned and depended. It gave me peace. I looked at the scripture from the perspective of God himself speaking peace into my life, because he knew exactly what I needed.

I have often said that if I had lost my mother a few years earlier, I wouldn't have been able to go on. The reason for this is simple. I wasn't strong enough in my faith to deal with such a loss at that time. I often relied on my mother more than I probably should have when I was younger, but when I lost her the ONLY person I could lean and depend on was GOD.

I probably should have lost my mind, but God kept me. One of the things that kept me going besides God was the memory of my mother. She was so happy that I was going to college to better myself and often told me how proud she was of me. I knew that in spite of her absence, she would want me to continue to pursue my dreams and I did so wholeheartedly.

If you are reading this book, it may be because you are currently dealing with your own obstacles, or you may have dealt with obstacles in the past, but you are struggling to move forward. Maybe you need to draw encouragement from someone else's story on this journey that we call life. Whatever the case maybe, this book is written specifically for you.

People often tell me how strong I am. They say that my life could be spiraling out of control, but you will never know because I don't show any signs of distress. I remember a conversation that I had with a friend when my mother passed, and he said to me that if he was in a similar situation, he didn't know how he would make it through. My response to that is, you never know how strong you are until you have no choice, but to be strong. To the people who are struggling to overcoming obstacles and to those who have gotten past the obstacles, but aren't sure how to move forward in life, I have good news for you. You will beat the odds and overcome whatever obstacles that you may be facing or have faced in the past. John 16:33 NIV says, "I have told you these things, so that in me you may have peace. In this world you will have trouble. But take heart! I have overcome the world." The Amplified Bible says, "I have told you these things, so that in me you may have [perfect] peace *and* confidence. In the world you have tribulation *and* trials *and* distress *and* frustration; but be of good cheer [take courage; be confident, certain, undaunted]! For I have overcome the world. [I have deprived it of power to harm you and have conquered it for you.]" Do you have perfect peace and confidence? Are you confident and certain of

God's word? Do you believe that God has deprived the world of its power to harm you? Do you believe that he has conquered the world for you? My sincere prayer is that the answers to these questions are yes, but if that isn't the case for you, then that's ok as well.

This book is to lift you up and encourage you, and with the help of God, I will be a blessing to your life. Truth is, all of us have been faced with situations or circumstances in life that became obstacles that we had to overcome. The important thing to remember is that we are not alone. We serve a God that is with us always even right now as you read this book. God is an ever-present help in the time of trouble. God is there to serve as counselor when you feel that there is no one to talk to or no one who understands. God is there to serve as a doctor when you need your broken heart mended. Whatever the case may be, God is there ALWAYS! Life is tough and you will face many obstacles, but the Good News is that you don't have to face them alone. God is for you, so it really doesn't matter who or what is against you. 1 Corinthians 15:57 says, "But thanks be to God! He gives us the victory through our Lord Jesus Christ." Isn't it wonderful to know that you have the victory over everything that you will face in this life? Get up and start to walk in your victory. In the end, you win!

Humble Beginnings

I was born and raised in Mobile, AL. To be a bit more specific, I grew up in a housing project which is affectionately known as Orange Grove or "The Grove." I grew up with very little and according to the standards of society, we were poor. My father passed when I was about 2 years old and I never really knew him or anything about him. I was raised by a single mother, who not only raised me, but four other siblings who are all girls. I look back now and wonder how she raised five children with little to no income. I applaud my mother because I truly believe she did the best that she could raising her children.

It wasn't easy growing up in the projects, but I made the most of it. I could have easily gotten caught up in a lifestyle that would have landed me in prison or in the cemetery. I thank God that I didn't. I hung around a lot of people who were "shining" and while the money, cars, and clothes were tempting, I knew that I didn't want it that way. There were only two ways out of that lifestyle and I wasn't willing to take either route.

I have seen people that I looked up to get caught up and throw away any chance of a decent life. I knew that if I had gone down that road, it would have broken my mother's heart, and I never wanted to do anything to hurt her. I have had family members that I love dearly write me off. It was said that I would never amount to much and that I would be dead or in prison if I continued on the same path. Hearing the people that I loved say this hurt me on so many levels, but instead of feeling sorry for myself and using it as a crutch, I used it to motivate me. I was determined to make good grades in school and take up an extracurricular activity to ensure that I wouldn't have any time to waste on unnecessary things that may have gotten me into trouble.

I don't have this amazing come-to-Jesus story, but what I do have is my testimony about how I was restored back unto Jesus Christ. I accepted Jesus Christ as my Lord and Savior when I was about 10 years old. Shortly after being baptized, I strayed away for about four years and during that time life taught me a lot. One Sunday morning, I was at home alone and God spoke to me and said, "Go back to the church." I was obedient and the following Sunday I attended church. I haven't looked back since, and I must say that it was the best decision that I have ever made. At an early age, I knew that getting an education and staying out of trouble would be my way out.

We all have had teachers ask us what we wanted to be when we grow up and initially my answer was scattered. This was because I didn't really start to narrow down exactly what I wanted to be until I was in middle school. That is when I started to grow fond of math and science. I was always good at science, but I struggled with math. I knew that I would have to find a way to become better at math if I wanted to specialize in anything engineering related. I have always said that I wanted to own my own engineering firm. While I didn't know it then, that dream would later become a reality.

I often look back over my life and realize that it is only by the grace of God that I am here today. It was often said that nothing good comes from the hood. There is even scripture in the Bible that backs this up. In John 1:45-46, Phillip, a follower of Christ found Nathanael and told him, "We have found the one Moses wrote about in the Law, and about whom the prophets also wrote- Jesus of Nazareth, the son of Joseph." "Nazareth! Can anything good come from there?" Nathanael asked. In society today, there are still people who think this way. I am living proof though, along with many others who have made something of their life despite their upbringing, that good things often come from the hood. I believe Jesus was the ultimate example of a good thing that came from the hood.

According to statistics, I was one of 54% to graduate from high school and in 2001 I had a 32.2% chance of going to prison. Those statistics alone are enough for me to realize that God had his hand on me and even when I didn't have sense enough to take care of myself, He was doing it for me. I often wonder why I didn't go down the wrong path. Why was I so different from the other people who lost their way along life's journey? The only thing that I could think of is God protected me from myself. He had a plan for my life far greater than anything that I could comprehend. Every person that still has breathe in his/her body has a purpose here on this earth, but one must be willing to seek God so he can reveal that purpose. God will not force anyone to accept him or serve him, but eventually every knee shall bow and every tongue shall confess that Jesus is Lord. That is a choice that you have to make on your own. That is why God gives us all free will. Proverbs 16:9 says "The heart of man plans his way, but the Lord establishes his steps." No matter where you are from or what you have done, God has a plan for your life. People may turn their backs on you and leave you to your own devices, but God will never leave you nor forsake you. He promised to be with you always, even until the end of the world. Jeremiah 29:11 says, "For I know the plans I have for you," declares the Lord, "plans to prosper you and not to harm you, plans to give you hope and a future." Get busy! Figure out what God's plan for your life is and walk in your destiny. Don't allow humble beginnings to close the door to success. Job 8:7 NIV says, "Your beginnings will seem humble, so prosperous will your future be."

Timing Is Everything

It was the summer of 2011 and I had recently finished the requirements for my Bachelor of Science Degree in Computer Science. Shortly after completing those requirements, I began my career at a very large corporation. This company wasn't new to me because I had interned there while I was still an undergraduate. This gave me a slight advantage over new graduates coming in with no previous experience in the corporate world. The learning curve wasn't as steep as it normally is for a new graduate entering the workforce.

After about a month-and-a-half on the job, I decided to leave the company and take a job with the government in the Washington D.C. area. I was often asked, "Why are you leaving the company?" Shortly after arriving, I quickly realized that there are people who are threatened by young, educated, black men with new ideas. I couldn't wrap my head around the idea that someone would try to hold you back purposely, so that they could get ahead. Now that I think back on the situation, I probably should have stayed at the company and worked through the situation. Instead of being patient and figuring out a solution to the problem, I left the company and took a job that I thought would be a better fit for me. It didn't take me very long to realize that I had moved hundreds of miles away for a job that ultimately didn't make me happy. After about six months on the job, I resigned and returned home to Mobile, AL.

When I returned to Mobile, little did I know that I would be in for a rude awakening. Someone that I expected to be there to support me until I figured out my next move basically deserted me when I needed them most. I thought to myself that if I had known that this was going to happen, I would have stayed in place until things got better. I would have been forced to either get an apartment or live in my car until I figured out my next move. At the time, I didn't want to exhaust what I had saved on an apartment because I didn't know how long I would be there. Or if I could even keep up with the cost associated with the apartment.

I was at my lowest point in my life and I didn't think that I could get any lower. Just when I thought that I may be sleeping in my car, God sent an angel to rescue me in the form of one of my in-laws. I was unemployed for about six months and this was one of the toughest times in my life. After going on many interviews for jobs and not getting hired, I was ready to end my search for employment. Suddenly, God turned my situation around. I had two jobs interviews with the same company and I never saw it coming. I was offered the job in a city that I had been trying to get to for months. What I had been trying to do for months, God did in a matter of hours.

How often do we proceed with decisions that we think are best for us without consulting God? We often forget that what we know (or what we think we know) doesn't even compare to God's depth of wisdom and knowledge. Isaiah 55:9 NIV says, "As the heavens are higher than the earth, so are my ways higher than your ways and my thoughts than your thoughts." The Bible reminds us that God's ways and thoughts are much higher than ours, and we can only understand small pieces of his plan for our lives. Our responsibility is to let God lead us and believe that all things work for the good of those who love him, who have been called according to his purpose. This doesn't mean that your life will be perfect and you will never face adversity. However, it does mean that when we face various trials and tribulations, they can have happy endings if we trust and obey God.

When you endure tough times, you can learn a lot about yourself. You can also learn a lot about your life and the role that God plays in your life. I now know that the only person in this world that I can depend on to never let me down is God. Before going through this storm, I can't say I knew that. The people that I expected to be there for me weren't and the people that I least expected to be there for me welcomed me with open arms. Your situation may seem obscure and you may not know how you are going to make it through, but I encourage you to keep on living. Continue to trust God with your life and watch him work it out. It may be tough, but don't quit! God is able to do exceeding abundantly above all that we ask or think, according to the power that works within us. Don't give up on something that you believe in, even if you are neglected or rejected. Keep doing your best and giving it your all. You never know how close to the blessing you really are. If you quit though, you will never know. Jeremiah 29:11 says, "For I know the plans I have for you," declares the Lord, "plans to prosper you and not to harm you, plans to give you hope and a future." There's no need for you to sit around and try to figure out how things are going to work out. Rest assured that God has a future planned for you beyond anything that you could ever imagine for yourself. Your situation may get worse before it gets better, but be confident and know that it will get better. We often want those instant "name it and claim it" blessings, but some of the best blessings are those that are delayed. Don't mistake a delayed blessing for a denial. Get ready to receive whatever it is that you are believing God for. Are you ready to receive your blessing? If you're not, I suggest that you get ready, because it's on the way.

When Life Knocks You Down, Seek God

There's a popular phrase that goes something like this, either you are entering a storm, exiting a storm, or about to go into a storm. Life happens to all of us and it's no respecter of person. No one is exempt from the troubles of this world. Psalms 34:19 NIV says, "The righteous person may have many troubles, but the Lord delivers him from them all." If life has not yet knocked you down, keep living. There are many things that we can do when life knocks us down, but what we should do is seek God.

I am reminded of a situation in my own life when I could have thrown in the towel and quit, but instead, I asked God for guidance and direction and he provided it. In August of 2013, I was fired from my job for standing up to my former employer for showing favoritism based on the color of one's skin. During that time, I didn't know how I would survive or where my next paycheck would come from. I remember praying to God and asking him to show me where to go from here. The answer didn't come instantly, but eventually God spoke to me and told me to start my own business. This was something that I didn't expect because I didn't know the first thing about business. Yet, it didn't mean that I couldn't take the time to learn. I embraced the process and it has caused me to grow tremendously. Sometimes God closes doors in our lives in order for us to grow. He knows that if he doesn't shake things up in our lives, we will never reach our full potential.

Job's story is an awesome example for us to follow when life knocks us down. Job lost everything that was important to him, but he still remained faithful to God. If you lost everything that had value to you, would you remain faithful to God? In spite of his loss, Job did not blame God for any of his misfortunes. Job 1:20-21 says, "At this, Job got up and tore his robe and shaved his head. Then he fell to the ground in worship and said: "Naked I came from my mother's womb, and naked I will depart. The Lord gave and the Lord has taken away; may the name of the Lord be praised."

It's important to realize that nothing that we have truly belongs to us. God is simply allowing us to be stewards over the things that we possess until his return. Job understood this perfectly and that's why he was able to worship God in spite of his loss. When God closes doors in our lives, we won't always know the reason that the door closed. But we can rest assured that God has a very good reason for closing the door. God has a plan for our lives that's far beyond anything we can comprehend with our human minds.

When life knocks you down, the enemy will try to convince you that God has forsaken you and that life is no longer worth living. You have to cast down the spirit of doubt and hopelessness, and stand on all that you know to be true about God. Sometimes that's going to be the only thing that keeps you going. When life knocks you down, there will be people who assume sin or wrong doing caused your downfall. I urge you to stay away from these people. They mean you no good and only desire to spread things about you that are simply not true. Job had to deal with this type of behavior from people that he considered friends. Can you imagine being accused of something that's simply not true by people you call friends? Eventually, God intervened on Job's behalf and got upset with Job's friends for making false assumptions. Job pleads with God on their behalf and God forgives them.

God blessed Job far beyond anything that he could have ever imagined. God restored Job's health, blessed him with twice as much as he had before, blessed him with new children, and an extremely long life. If God can do that much for Job, then how much more can he do for you? You may be going through right now and you may not see a way out of your circumstances. It may seem that no matter where you turn, there's trouble on every side and things appear to be getting worst. I want to encourage you to hang in there a little while longer because God will restore unto you everything that you lost. 1 Peter 5:10 says, "And the God of all grace, who called you to his eternal glory in Christ, after you have suffered a little while, will himself restore you and make you strong, firm and steadfast." Often times we want what God has for us, but we don't want to go through anything to get it. Psalms 34:19-20 NIV tells us, "The righteous person may have many troubles, but the Lord delivers him from them all; he protects all his bones, not one of them will be broken." Isn't it wonderful to know that no matter what you go through, God has you covered? When the burdens of this world come bearing down on you, it's wonderful to know that God will protect you. Are you ready for God to restore unto you what the locust have eaten up in your life? God promises us in his word that he will restore unto us whatever was eaten up in our lives by the locust. Can you feel things starting to turn in your favor? Are you ready to conquer the things in your life that were once pitfalls? Now that God has restored the things that you once lost, make the choice to live again. God's desire (wish) is that you enjoy life and have it in great abundance. Don't put it off any longer! Take him up on his offer!

Forgiving Those Who Betray You

Forgiving someone can be a very difficult thing to do. This is especially true if you feel that they betrayed you. Forgiveness isn't so much for the person that betrayed you; it's really for you. I don't know if you have ever held a grudge against someone, but if you haven't, let me tell you that it isn't a good thing. I have held grudges against people and they turned me into someone that I didn't recognize. I was very bitter towards those people and couldn't even bring myself to speak to them. When you can't bring yourself to speak someone, there are some issues within yourself that you need to resolve. You may be saying to yourself, "This person hurt me to my core! There is no way that I can forgive them." The good news is there is a way that you can find it in your heart to forgive them, but you must have a willing spirit towards forgiveness. God has given us specific instructions when it comes to forgiving others. Mark 11:25 NIV says, "And when you stand praying, if you hold anything against anyone, forgive them, so that your Father in heaven may forgive you your sins."

It's impossible to hold a grudge against someone else and still be in God's good graces. You can't expect to receive God's blessings holding onto hate and malice in your heart for another person. I compare holding a grudge to full hands. How will you receive anything or anyone if your hands are full? You can't! Because there is no room for anything else. Love and forgiveness go hand in hand. There is no love without forgiveness and vice versa. 1 John 4:20 NIV says, "Whoever claims to love God yet hates a brother or sister is a liar. For whoever does not love their brother and sister, whom they have seen, cannot love God, whom they have not seen." I realized that God is love and that he wasn't pleased with the hatred that I had in my heart for those people, so I forgave them. After forgiving those people, I had so much peace. It felt as if there was a huge weight lifted from my shoulders. If you are holding a grudge against anyone, forgive them. Forgiveness will remove the anger and hatred that you have towards the person that offended you. An unforgiving heart puts our daily walk with God at risk. The Holy Spirit can't dwell where there is sin, and bitterness (unforgiving spirit) is a sin. If God can forgive you for your many transgressions, then you can forgive the person that you are holding that grudge against. In this life, people are going to do things to you or say things about you that hurt you. You must get in the habit of forgiving people over and over again.

Matthew 18: 21-22 says, "Then Peter came to Jesus and asked, "Lord, how many times shall I forgive my brother or sister who sins against me? Up to seven times?" Jesus answered, "I tell you, not seven times, but seventy-seven times." Often times, we are hurt by people that we love and that makes it very hard for us to forgive. However, if we truly love those people like we say we do, then we will forgive those people. You may be saying to yourself "If the situation had been the other way around, I would have never done anything like that to him or her.

The truth is, everyone's intentions aren't as pure as yours. In spite of that person's intentions we can't hold on to what they have done to us. 1 Corinthians 13:4-6 NIV says, "Love is patient, love is kind. It does not envy, it does not boast, it is not proud. It does not dishonor others, it is not self-seeking, it is not easily angered, it keeps no record of wrongs. Love does not delight in evil but rejoices with the truth." Think about everything that you have ever done that was ungodly. Now picture God telling you that he's not going to forgive you for any of it. How would you feel if God didn't forgive you for the sins that you committed? I can imagine that you wouldn't feel very good at all. The good news is God keeps no record of our wrongdoings, so when we ask for forgiveness, he grants it at that very moment. Isaiah 43:25 says, "I, even I, am he who blots out your transgressions, for my own sake, and remembers your sins no more." If you don't forgive those that sin against you, how can you expect to be forgiven? Matthew 6:14-15 NIV says, "For if you forgive other people when they sin against you, your heavenly Father will also forgive you. But if you do not forgive others their sins, your Father will not forgive your sins."

The first step to forgiving others is the willingness to forgive. I encourage you today to allow God to begin to heal your broken heart. If there is someone that you know you haven't forgiven, then I urge you to do so. The next thing that you should do is sit down and talk to that person (privately) and let them know how their betrayal affected you. Matthew 18:15-17 NIV gives us guidance on how to handle the reconciliation process. It says, "If your brother or sister sins, go and point out their fault, just between the two of you. If they listen to you, you have won them over. But if they will not listen, take one or two others along, so that 'every matter may be established by the testimony of two or three witnesses.' If they still refuse to listen, tell it to the church; and if they refuse to listen even to the church, treat them as you would a pagan or a tax collector." The best that you can do is try and make it right. If that attempt fails, then let them know that you still love them. Don't allow something that's caused you so much hurt and pain to continue to take up unnecessary space in your life. Move on with your life!

Pressing Forward In spite of Criticism

Have you ever embarked on a new journey that you were extremely excited about? Yet when you decided to share the details of this new journey with others, you quickly realized that those people weren't as happy for you as you thought they would be. I am remind of an instance in my own life that happened around the time that I started my business a few years ago. A situation similar to the one that I just described happened to me and I must say that it caught me off guard.

I had gone to lunch with a person that I expected to offer helpful advice, but instead the only thing that I received from this person was questions and criticism. I was being asked questions about things that were far from my mind at the time. After sitting through all of these questions, this person starts to question whether I was even qualified to be the owner of a business. I proceeded to tell this person that my degree and years of professional experience was enough to qualify me to run my business. Though I had every right to respond to this criticism harshly, I decided that it was best for me to show humility in this instance. Proverbs 15:1 NIV says, "A gentle answer turns away wrath, but a harsh word stirs up anger." I left that restaurant knowing that I can't share what's going on in my life with everyone. Even those that we think would be a great resource for advice, often times aren't happy for us. Needless to say, I didn't let all of the questions and criticism stop me from pursing my dream of being an entrepreneur. In August of 2015, I will be celebrating my two year business anniversary. Proverbs 17:24 NIV says, "A discerning person keeps wisdom in view, but a fool's eyes wander to the ends of the earth." You have to remember that you can't tell big dreams or plans to small-minded people. They simply won't comprehend them. Their lack of comprehension often turns into doubt and criticism that you simply don't need. Your goals and dreams for your life should be so big that you have to consult with God daily to achieve them. After all, God tells us in his word that he knows the plans that he has for our lives. Jeremiah 29:11 NIV says, "For I know the plans I have for you," declares the Lord, "plans to prosper you and not to harm you, plans to give you hope and a future." God can be trusted and I am a witness to that. If you are facing criticism today, I urge you to continue to press forward and consult with God along the way. He will never put more on you than you can bear. There is a popular saying that goes something like this, "God gives his toughest battles to his strongest soldiers." If you are facing a tough battle, I want to challenge you to stay in the fight. If God didn't think you were strong enough to endure it, then he wouldn't have allowed you to go through it. 1 Corinthians 10:13 NIV says, "No temptation has overtaken you except what is common to mankind. And God is faithful; he will not let you be tempted beyond what you can bear. But when you are tempted, he will also provide a way out so that you can endure it." Don't allow someone else's criticism to keep you from pursuing the things that your heart desires.

People fear the things they don't understand or have the courage to do. So if someone is questioning you or criticizing your decision to step out on faith, chances are they don't have the nerve to do something that they feel is frightening. They are simply trying to hold you back because of the fear within themselves. Whatever God has placed on your heart to do, I challenge you to step out on faith and do it. God doesn't do things just for the sake of time; if he has given it to you then there is a reason for him doing so.

Many of us have different desires of the heart and gifts that we have allowed to lie dormant because someone criticized us or told us that we can't do it. I urge you today to start living out those desires and using those gifts that God has blessed you with. If your gift is to preach and teach, then get busy doing so. If your heart's desire is to become an entrepreneur, then I urge you to start figuring out what type of business makes sense for you. You may be saying to yourself, "I don't have a platform to use my gift or I don't have the connections needed to start a business." If you don't have a platform, then create one. There are so many ways in this day and age to ensure that your voice is heard. Stop worrying about what you don't have and shift your focus on what you do have. And that's the gift(s) that God has blessed you with. When the time is right, God will allow you to encounter what you need in order to be successful. Romans 8:31 NIV says, "What, then, shall we say in response to these things? If God is for us, who can be against us? "

If you are like me, then you often wonder how God's going to work things out in your life. I have learned that some things aren't for us to know. God wants to blow your mind with the blessing that he has in store for you. Romans 8:28 NIV says, "And we know that in all things God works for the good of those who love him, who have been called according to his purpose." Be encouraged! Everything will work out just fine. Continue to walk along the path that you know God has designed especially for you and watch how God change things. Are you ready for God to move in your life? Ready or not, a move of God is coming!

Being Content in Every Situation

Are you worried about what might happen in your future? Or do you doubt your ability to be successful? Are you unsure of other people's feelings toward you? If any of these questions pertain to you, then I have good news for you. The Bible has given us an awesome example in regards to the outlook that we should have when these type of questions arise and the peace that we should have when dealing with questions of this nature. This example comes in the form of the apostle Paul, who wrote much of the New Testament in the Bible and possessed a solid viewpoint when it came to the believer worrying about things. Philippians 4:6 NIV says, "Do not be anxious about anything, but in every situation, by prayer and petition, with thanksgiving, present your requests to God." Paul is instructing the believer not to be "anxious about anything". Take a moment to process those words. Are you worried about something today that you probably shouldn't be worrying about? Paul is encouraging us as believers not to worry about anything.

If Paul can utter those words, then we should listen. Paul was in prison when he wrote this letter to the church at Philippi. While in prison, Paul endured being beaten, being locked up in chains, and being separated from his family and his friends. Paul didn't complain about his circumstances, but instead he praised God. Would you be able to praise God in spite of enduring many trials and tribulations? Paul not only dealt with being thrown in prison, but he had a physical condition (which he referred to as a thorn in his flesh) that he repeatedly asked God to cure, yet God decided not to relieve him of this ailment.

When Paul wasn't imprisoned, he was being shipwrecked, bitten by a poisonous snake, and stoned by people who didn't appreciate him spreading the gospel of Jesus Christ. Ultimately, Paul's belief in Jesus Christ got him beheaded. We shouldn't only listen to Paul, but we should emulate his outlook in our own lives. People's opinions or feelings toward Paul weren't important to him. The only thing important to Paul was that God loved him and had a plan for his life. You can be assured that God loves you too. And just like he had a plan for Paul's life, he has one for yours as well that doesn't involve you worrying about how things will work out.

Stay focused, maintain a positive outlook and everything will be fine. Will time stop if you don't become rich tomorrow? Will the earth no longer spin on its axis if you lose your job? Will babies no longer be born? Will the rooster no longer crow in the morning? What are these things compared to God's love for you and his wonderful plan for your life? None of these things can even compare to what God has in store for your future. God has never said that you wouldn't go through trials and tribulations. In fact, his word tells us that many are the afflictions of the righteous, but the lord delivers him out of them all. Based on his circumstances, it would have been easy for Paul to throw in the towel and lose hope. But instead of the latter, Paul sought God. God doesn't honor doubt or fear, but he does honor faith. James 1:6-8 NIV says, "But when you ask, you must believe and not doubt, because the one who doubts is like a wave of the sea, blown and tossed by the wind. That person should not expect to receive anything from the Lord. Such a person is double-minded and unstable in all they do." When God decided not to remove the thorn from Paul's flesh, he learned something very important. God doesn't always remove the things in our lives that cause worry and concern, but he does give of his grace so that we may continue to live our lives in spite of these things. 2 Corinthians 12:9 NIV says, "But he said to me, "My grace is sufficient for you, for my power is made perfect in weakness." Therefore I will boast all the more gladly about my weaknesses, so that Christ's power may rest on me." Truly, there is nothing too hard for God. The things of this world don't bother God, because God has overcome the world. God is victorious over all things and because you are a child of God's, you are victorious also. Use this new understanding of God's power to convert the time that you spend worrying into a chance to search for God's peace and viewpoint. While Paul was imprisoned, instead of worrying about things that were beyond his control, he wrote letters of instruction and encouragement to believers and to friends. Paul wrote these letters to the Christians in Rome, the church in Corinth, the churches in southern Galatia, the church at Ephesus, the Christians at Philippi, the church at Colosse, the church at Thessalonica, and to friends Timothy, Philemon, and Titus. Whatever is going on in your life right now, don't spend time worrying about how and when things are going to work themselves out. Be the best you can be, right where you are. Seek God and develop a plan to help you move forward with your life. It's amazing how a single step in the right direction can lead to a turn of events in your life. Always talk to God about your life and the things that you are dealing with. Seek God's plan for your life and his wisdom for your future. When the road gets rough, ask God for that peace that transcends all understanding. Trust and believe that God has you covered and he will bring you out. Matthew 6:34 NIV says, "Therefore do not worry about tomorrow, for tomorrow will worry about itself. Each day has enough trouble of its own.

Trusting God

It was the spring of 2007, and I had recently started the second semester of my freshman year of college. I was coming off of a wonderful 1st semester, in which my GPA was a 3.6. I was on an emotional high and feeling as if nothing could go wrong. A few weeks into the second semester, it seemed as if everything had started to go wrong. I have never been great at mathematics, but my major(Computer Science) required me to take very high level math courses like Calculus I,II, and III. In order for me to begin taking Calculus, I had to pass these pre-requisites that were called pre-calculus algebra/trigonometry. When I begin the course, I quickly found out that the course was hard. While the instructor was teaching the course, I was able to comprehend and follow along with what was being taught. But when it was time to take the test, my mind went blank which resulted in me failing the test. During this time, I was really struggling to understand the concepts. I went back to my dorm room and seriously considered dropping out of college and returning home to Mobile, AL. All of these negative thoughts entered my mind about quitting and throwing in the towel, because of the course's level of difficulty. It was like the enemy was rejoicing in my struggles. I remember thinking to myself, "There's really nothing in Mobile for me, but I want to get out of this situation so bad that I am willing to return home and figure the rest out when I get there." Before I made a decision, I prayed and asked God for guidance. And when I begin to pray, God spoke to me and told me to trust him and everything would be fine. I took God's advice, trusted him and everything worked out just fine. Not only did I pass that class, but I passed every other mathematics class that I took during the course of my college career.

Are you struggling with something that has you thinking about throwing in the towel? If so, then I urge you to give it to God and trust that he will work it out for you. Don't allow things that are beyond your control to beat you down. Instead, trust the one who is in control of all things to change your circumstances. Proverbs 3:5-6 NIV says, "Trust in the Lord with all your heart and lean not on your own understanding; in all your ways submit to him, and he will make your paths straight."

Often, we are hurt by people, or we are let down by people that we thought would be there for us, and this causes us to question whether a person will keep their word. If we are not careful, this will spill over into our spiritual lives and we will find ourselves questioning God. Doubt and pride will cause us to develop a "If you want something done right, do it yourself attitude." This type of attitude is dangerous, because in your mind, no one will ever get it quite right. God won't even be able to live up to your standards in your mind, because his ways aren't your ways and his thoughts aren't your thoughts. If this is something that you are struggling with, then pray to God and ask him to help you with your unbelief. Proverbs 28:26 NIV says, "He who trusts in himself is a fool, but he who walks in wisdom is kept safe."

God is available to us 24 hours a day, seven days a week. There's no longer a need for someone else to go to God on our behalf. We can now do that ourselves and learn from God how he wants us to live. We can learn to hear from God through the reading of his holy word. Romans 12:2 NIV says, "Do not conform any longer to the pattern of this world, but be transformed by the renewing of your mind. Then you will be able to test and prove what God's will is--his good, pleasing and perfect will."

We have to make it a habit to study the word of God daily. The more time you spend studying God's word, the stronger your relationship with him becomes. Once our relationship with God becomes stronger, we can then hear him speak to our hearts. We will no longer have to make decisions based on what we think or feel. We will now be able to make decisions based on what God laid on our hearts. John 8:47 NIV says, "Whoever belongs to God hears what God says. The reason you do not hear is that you do not belong to God." When we put our feelings and desires to the side, and focus on what God is telling us to do, only then can we fully trust him.

Trusting God fully with your life will lead to many wonderful blessings. God will take you places that you never would have been able to go on your own.

When you don't understand what's going on in your life, will you trust God? Will you do your best and trust God to do the rest? II Timothy 1:7 NIV says, "For the Spirit God gave us does not make us timid, but gives us power, love and self-discipline." The Amplified Bible says, "For God did not give us a spirit of timidity (of cowardice, of craven and cringing and fawning fear), but [He has given us a spirit] of power and of love and of calm *and* well-balanced mind *and* discipline *and* self-control." When we worry and allow fear to control our lives, then we are basically telling God that our fears are bigger than our faith. I know that you aren't with me and that you can't help me through this. Ephesians 3:20 NIV says, "Now to him who is able to do immeasurably more than all we ask or imagine, according to his power that is at work within us," God is able to do things far beyond the comprehension of our human minds. The question is though, what will you trust God to do in your life?

It's Really Not about You

Nothing that you go through in this life is about you. Often, we go through things in this life for two reasons. The first reason is so that God can get the glory and the second reason is so that we can help someone else overcome what they may be going through. There have been many instances in my own life when I have gone through things, and shortly after the storm passed in my life, someone reached out to me for advice, because they were going through a similar situation. My experience with the situation enabled me to give them sound advice about how to get through the difficult time that they were facing.

In this life, you will have troubles. You won't always be comfortable, happy, successful, or free from pain. Life is not about you; it's about God. He intends for you to become the man or woman that he called you to be. You may be saying to yourself, "How can you confidently make this statement?" Paul's response in II Corinthians 12:9-10 says "But he said to me, "My grace is sufficient for you, for my power is made perfect in weakness." Therefore I will boast all the more gladly about my weaknesses, so that Christ's power may rest on me. That is why, for Christ's sake, I delight in weaknesses, in insults, in hardships, in persecutions, in difficulties. For when I am weak, then I am strong." Paul lived by this for the rest of his days and it would be helpful to us if we adopted it and applied it to our lives as well. When we brag about how well we are doing in life, we make the false assumption that it is by our own strength that we are blessed. We take the credit for our success and never give credit to whom it's actually due. But when we brag about how God is keeping us in spite of unemployment, our broken spirits, and our inabilities, then we are giving God the credit for what he has done in our lives.

Let's take a closer look at Paul in II Corinthians 12:9-10. Paul embraced his weaknesses, insults, difficulties, and hardships. But when we are faced with these things in our lives, we often dread going through them. Paul didn't mind enduring these things, because he understood that God give us his divine strength in our time of weakness as humans. And knowing that made Paul reverence God even more. We can learn a lot from Paul's unselfish humility. Though he endured many trials and tribulations, he never complained about his circumstances. How often do we go through things and complain? It can be the simplest thing, but yet we still complain about it. "It's hot in here!" "I am tired of standing in this line, I have been here all day." "They should shorten my work schedule, because I never get to spend time with my family." If the room was extremely cold, you would want them to turn the air down. Or if there were no lines and people were allowed to come and go as they please, then you would complain about there not being any structure. Or if you were taken off of the schedule completely, then you would complain about how your hours were cut. We have to learn to be content in whatever situation that we are in, because things could always be worse. Now being content in your situation doesn't mean that you sit around and let life pass you by. But what it does mean is that you have peace within while you are working through your circumstances.

Jesus Christ was the ultimate example of how selfless we should be when it comes to God's will for our lives. Although he didn't have to, Jesus willingly died to pay the price for the sins of the whole world. This was truly a selfless act and Paul allowed this act to permeate his life. If we truly want to learn how to be content in every situation, then we should develop an attitude of selflessness. Before we start spreading this attitude to the world, we should start at home with our family, friends, and neighbors. We should then exemplify this example on our jobs, and if we own a business, we should exemplify it with our clients. You will be surprised by the impact this type of attitude will have on people. Paul urged the believer to have an attitude of grateful acceptance. Paul didn't hold back on his views of how believers should bond with one another. Philippians 2:14-15 NIV says, "Do everything without grumbling or arguing, so that you may become blameless and pure, "children of God without fault in a warped and crooked generation." Then you will shine among them like stars in the sky." Paul sought an attitude of grateful acceptance, without disputes and bickering. He pleaded with the believers, urging them to have pure joy. This kind of joy spreads easily! Have you adopted an attitude of grateful acceptance? Is your life filled with pure joy? Do you have an attitude of selflessness? If the answer is no to any of these questions, I want to encourage you to ask God for an attitude of selflessness, an attitude of grateful acceptance, and pure joy. An attitude of selflessness leads to a life of happiness that's filled with joy.

Walking In Your Destiny

We are all born with a gift(s) and that gift often times translate into the things that we are passionate about in life--the kind of things that we would do all day if we were able. When you are truly passionate about something, you will do it for free. No one will have to pay you to do it, because you enjoy it so much. The pressures of life often cause us to forget about the things that we are passionate about and we totally neglect our purpose in life. It's extremely easy to get caught up in doing what it takes to keep up. Let me explain a bit further!

Often, we work long hours to earn a pay check, because we know that bills have to be paid. Or we enroll in school because we feel the need to get more education to advance our careers. But what about life beyond the things that you absolutely have to do? Are you doing the things that you love and that truly make you happy? Or are you doing the things that will look good on a resume and make you popular according to the world's standards? What are you doing outside of your everyday norm to challenge yourself to become a better you? In other words, are you living up to life's standards? Or are you following God's purpose for your life? Whether you believe it or not, God has a plan for your life. And he equipped you with your gift(s) so that they may be used for the up building of his kingdom. Your gifts and the things that you are passionate about are often tied to your destiny; the reason for God creating you and placing you here on earth.

I am reminded of a time in my own life when I ran from the calling that God had placed on my life. People would always tell me that I had a calling on my life, but I never gave it any real thought until God revealed to me his plan for my life. But even when God revealed it to me, I didn't want to accept it. It took a chance encounter with God in my dorm room at about 3 A.M. in the morning to change my outlook about God's calling on my life. I realized that I was being extremely selfish and I wasn't going to have any peace until I surrendered my will to God's will. Am I perfect? Of course not! I still make mistakes daily. Paul says it best in Philippians 3:12 NIV, "Not that I have already obtained all this, or have already arrived at my goal, but I press on to take hold of that for which Christ Jesus took hold of me." The Amplified Bible says, "Not that I have now attained [this ideal], or have already been made perfect, but I press on to lay hold of (grasp) *and* make my own, that for which Christ Jesus (the Messiah) has laid hold of me *and* made me His own." I have discovered that life's unfavorable situations have caused many believers to accept the low moments in life as their final destination. We are more than conquerors through him that loves us. Don't allow the enemy to have his way in your life when God wants you to succeed and has promised you success. If much of your life is boring, difficult, or unpleasant, then you may not be walking in your destiny. Are you willing to leave behind what you are currently doing to follow God plan for your life? God's plan for you is to experience a life that's lively and fits perfectly together with the gifts that he has given you.

Don't live your life in a sequence of aimless events. Live your life on purpose and live it passionately. What's stopping you from embracing your destiny? Fear is one of the major factors that stop us from embracing our destiny. We have trouble dealing with what we don't understand. Fear shouldn't cripple us, but it's still present in many Christians lives today. What are we afraid of? Are we afraid of being successful? Or what others make think of us once we become successful? Or is our fear of failure so great that it prevents us from launching out into the deep? Deuteronomy 31:6 NIV says, "Be strong and courageous. Do not be afraid or terrified because of them, for the Lord your God goes with you; he will never leave you nor forsake you." If we would seek God in all of our endeavors and trust him when he tells us to do something, we would find it a bit easier to accomplish our goals in life, because of the provisions that he has for us. Psalms 37:3-4 NIV says, "Trust in the Lord and do good; dwell in the land and enjoy safe pasture. Take delight in the Lord, and he will give you the desires of your heart."

Self-Esteem is another factor that prevents us from embracing our destiny. Many of us allow what others say and think about us to change our perspective of who we are in the eyes of the lord. The word of God says Jesus answered, "It is written: 'Man shall not live on bread alone, but on every word that comes from the mouth of God." In other words, the only thing that matters is what God says about you. Man's opinion of you is simply irrelevant, because God has the final word when it comes to your life. Often times, people can see your destiny even before you can. And if that person doesn't desire that you succeed, then they are going to offer words of discouragement. Those type of people are called destiny killers and I urge you to stay away from people like that. These kind of people will often pose questions like; are you really going to do that? Why not do something that provides more security? No one else is doing anything like that; why should you? If God has placed something on your heart that you know he has purposed you to do, then I want to encourage you to go for it.

Using the Gifts God Has Given You

If you received a gift from someone who was known for selecting the perfect present for the people that they purchased gifts for, would you be excited to find out what the package contained? Would this gift be something that you would want to start using right away? God gives many people the perfect gifts, but they never bother to use them for their intended purpose. They often say, "I have to work on Sunday, I can't sing in the choir." Or "I can't give up my full time job to go into ministry, because it won't pay the bills." God has given us all gifts, talents, and abilities. These gifts, talents, and abilities make you who you are and distinguish you from others. God gave you these gifts so that they can benefit others, not yourself. There is more to life than just paying bills, making money, and dying. We are all a part of the body of Christ and each part of the body has a purpose. You are important to God, and your gift matter to him. Romans 12:4-8 NIV says "For just as each of us has one body with many members, and these members do not all have the same function, so in Christ we, though many, form one body, and each member belongs to all the others. We have different gifts, according to the grace given to each of us. If your gift is prophesying, then prophesy in accordance with your faith; if it is serving, then serve; if it is teaching, then teach; if it is to encourage, then give encouragement; if it is giving, then give generously; if it is to lead, do it diligently; if it is to show mercy, do it cheerfully." Whatever your gift may be, use it to serve others. 1 Peter 4:10 NIV says "Each of you should use whatever gift you have received to serve others, as faithful stewards of God's grace in its various forms." You are the manager of the gift(s) that God has entrusted to you, and he expects you to be a faithful and wise steward over them. 1 Corinthians 4:2 says, "Now it is required that those who have been given a trust must prove faithful." Are you using the gifts that God has given you? Or are you simply allowing them to sit up and collect dust? Are you using your gifts to benefit other? Or are you using your gifts for personal gain? (Simply benefitting yourself) When God gives us a gift, he expects us to use it. Your gifts are like muscles. If you use them, then they will grow, but if you don't use them, then you will lose them. I am reminded of a parable in the Bible about the servants with the ten talents in Luke

19. Each of the servants were given talents, but not all of the servants used their talents. Unfortunately, for one of the servants his talent was taken away and given to someone else. If we don't use what God has given us, then he will take ours a way as well and give it to someone else. But if we use our talents to glorify God, then he will give us more. If we use our time to glorify God, then he will bless us with more. If we use our influence to glorify God, then he will increase our influence. God will reward you for your faithfulness.

Do you know the answers to these questions? If not, then I suggest that you first consult God and ask him to reveal your gifts to you. Next, I suggest that you sit down and create a list of things that you do very well. Your gifts are often tied directly to the things that you are passionate about. Using your God-given talents is one of the most satisfying things that you will ever do. Doing what God created you to do often gives you a deep sense of purpose. It also allows you to become closer to the gift giver and to be grateful to God for the talents that he has instilled in you. There's nothing more beautiful than the Creator and the creation working together. If you are currently neglecting your gift, then make the decision today to begin putting it to use. It's never too late! Don't be envious of someone else's gift. Use what God has blessed you with to accomplish his will for your life. James 1:17 NIV says, "Every good and perfect gift is from above, coming down from the Father of the heavenly lights, who does not change like shifting shadows." Are you dissatisfied with where you are in life? Are you miserable on your current job or in your career? If you answered yes to any of these questions, then God may have another plan for your life. Seek guidance through prayer and scripture and ask God to reveal to you his plan for your life right now.

If you are in a situation and it's bringing you nothing but misery, then I suggest that you change your circumstances. The situation is never going to get better if you don't do something to change it. James 2:17 NIV says, "In the same way, faith by itself, if it is not accompanied by action, is dead." Often, people see things in us that we may not even notice ourselves. If people are constantly commenting on your talent or telling you how well you do something, then you should take note. God may be trying to tell you something through those people. I am not urging you to take advice from people about talents and gifts that you know you don't have, but if what people are complimenting you on lines up with what God has revealed to you, then it would be wise to consider. What's stopping you from using what God has gifted you with? Start today! And begin to walk in your purpose.

Get Ready For Your Comeback

Setbacks and disappointments have the potential to become a catastrophe in the people's lives in which they occur... How do you handle the disappointments that life hand to you? Many people internalize them and harbor them in their hearts where they cause them great pain, worry, and despair. Other take a different approach and share disappointments with friends, relatives, spiritual leaders, or counselors. If we are not prepared to deal with setbacks and disappointments, they can become permanent fixtures in our lives. You may be saying to yourself, "How do I prepare myself to deal with setbacks and disappointments?" We should talk to God about our disappointments and seek his guidance about how to overcome them. James 5:13 NIV says, "Is anyone among you in trouble? Let them pray. Is anyone happy? Let them sing songs of praise." When dealing with a setback, it's important to identify what's in your control and what isn't in your control. Don't spend time agonizing about things that you can't do anything about. You can't move forward with your life focusing on your setbacks and disappointments. When you focus on what you want your life to become going forward, then you can move on with your life and accomplish great things. Don't despise setbacks and disappointments as they are often God's way of redirecting your path in life. Everyone goes through setbacks in life, but it's important to look past those roadblocks and focus on what God has in store for your future. If you want to begin working towards what God has planned for your future, ask yourself these questions: What did God put you here to do? What can I do differently in my life to keep another setback from occurring? What shorts term goals do I want to accomplish over the next three, six, and twelve months? How can I use my setback as a learning experience? The answers to these questions can serve as a guide to you in your quest to begin working towards God's plans for your future. Philippians 1:6 NIV says, "Being confident of this, that he who began a good work in you will carry it on to completion until the day of Christ Jesus." You determine whether you are going to be a success or a failure. That decision is yours to make. You have to decide that you are going to press forward in spite of your setbacks and disappointments. Anyone who has ever succeeded at something knows that the secret to success is making the decision to be successful. Once you decide that you are going to accomplish something and you actually set your mind to it, then no one can stop you from achieving anything that you set out to do.

Habakkuk 2:2-3 NIV says, "then the Lord replied: Write down the revelation and make it plain on tablets so that a herald may run with it. For the revelation awaits an appointed time; it speaks of the end and will not prove false. Though it linger, wait for it; it will certainly come and will not delay." A decision without direction leads to a dead end, and direction without vision leads to a lot of confusion. Once you make up your mind that you want to achieve a goal, you must take the car out of park, shift the vehicle to drive and go. The vehicle in this instance is you. Unfortunately, many people never act on their decisions. While they have every intention to change their circumstances and achieve their goals, they lack the persistence and determination that is required to complete the task. When you decide to act on your decisions, you take accountability for achieving your goals. Remember, you may not be responsible for your setbacks and your disappointments, but you are responsible for how you respond to them. Do you have what it takes to reach your goals? What are you willing to do in order to achieve your goals? How badly do you want your situation to change? In order to reach your goals, you have to consistently strive to achieve success, even if it involves some degree of difficulty or risk. While taking risk can be intimidating, (especially after setbacks) it's absolutely necessary if you want to accomplish anything in life. The truth is, everything in life involves some type of risk, but if you step out on faith, and act on those things that God placed on your heart, then the rewards for those risks can be great. Hebrews 11:6 NIV says, "And without faith it is impossible to please God, because anyone who comes to him must believe that he exists and that he rewards those who earnestly seek him." No one is exempt from adverse situations in life, so the question isn't if a setback will occur, the question is when a setback occurs, and when a setback occurs, you need to make the decision to view it as an opportunity, rather than a problem. Make a decision about what you are going to do to resolve the issue and focus on solving the problem. A setback is simply a chance to go in a different direction and only those who don't embrace that chance fail. Are you ready for your comeback? If not, then I suggest that you get ready, because things are beginning to turn in your favor. You may have been down, but you are not out. It may not look like much now, but hang in there. Your situation will get better. Be encouraged! And get ready to start enjoying life again.

God Is Always There

We all go through tough times in life, and during those time, there are moments when we feel like giving up. We get discouraged and don't feel like continuing to fight the battles of life. No matter what we go through, we have to remember that God is always there for us. There may be times in our life when we feel like we are sinking in quicksand and getting nowhere fast. When you have been in your circumstances for a while, life can sometimes drain all of the energy out of you and make it hard for you to continue life's journey. If this describes your situation, then be encouraged because God is for you! He is by your side, even right now as you read these words. God is always thinking of you, encouraging you, loving you, and supporting you. Isn't it wonderful to know that you serve a God that's always there for you? Life happens to the best of us. But we have to keep pressing forward even though we don't understand what God is doing in our lives.

Sometimes problems arise in our lives, and it seems as if there is no way to avoid them. No matter how hard we try to keep our lives free from problems, they always seem to find their way in. Romans 8:28 NIV says, "And we know that in all things God works for the good of those who love him, who have been called according to his purpose." God is very consistent and we can count on him to be the same today, tomorrow, and forever more. He doesn't just offer his love and comfort to us when we are doing everything right and our feelings toward him are perfect. He offers it in spite of us. When we walk away from God, he still loves us. When we turn our backs on God, he still loves us. When we decide that we will no longer serve him and began to chase the things of this world, he still loves us. The Bible tells us that nothing can separate us from the love of God. Romans 8:38-39 says, "For I am convinced that neither death nor life, neither angels nor demons, neither the present nor the future, nor any powers, neither height nor depth, nor anything else in all creation, will be able to separate us from the love of God that is in Christ Jesus our Lord." As Christians, we often feel that we will live a life free from worry and stress because of our relationship with God. The deeds that we do for God doesn't exempt us from the sorrows of life. We have to endure our circumstances just like someone who isn't saved. What separates the Christian and the non-believer is a risen savior that we can count on to help us endure our circumstances.

I am reminded of the Prophet Elijah and how God was with him when Queen Jezebel threatened his life. God used Elijah to help prove to the worshippers of the false God Baal that he was the one true and living God. After the worshippers of Baal had prepared an offering to their God and prayed to him to consume it with fire, nothing happened. After Elijah prepared his offering to God and said his prayer to God, the Bible says "Then the fire of the Lord fell and burned up the sacrifice, the wood, the stones and the soil, and also licked up the water in the trench." During this time, it hadn't rained in Israel for three years and the country was experiencing a major drought. After he proved that God was lord of all, Elijah told King Ahab to "Go, eat and drink, for there is the sound of a heavy rain." The Bible says that while Ahab was eating, Elijah went up to the top of Mount Carmel to pray. Elijah told the servant that was with him, "Go and look toward the sea." He went up and looked. "There is nothing there," he said. Seven times Elijah said, "Go back." When the servant went back the seventh time, he saw a cloud approaching, which he described as a man's hand. Elijah said to the servant, "Go and tell Ahab, 'Hitch up your chariot and go down before the rain stops you." 1 Kings 18:46 says, "The power of the Lord came on Elijah and, tucking his cloak into his belt, he ran ahead of Ahab all the way to Jezreel." God was not only with Elijah when Queen Jezebel was trying to kill him, but he was with him when he ran ahead of Ahab to get to Jezreel. When we stand for God and do the things that he requires of us, he will be with us. Even in the presence of imminent danger, God is always there. When Elijah learned that Jezebel was serious about taking his life, the Bible says, "Elijah was afraid and ran for his life. When he came to Beersheba in Judah, he left his servant there, while he himself went a day's journey into the wilderness. He came to a broom bush, sat down under it and prayed that he might die. "I have had enough, Lord," he said. "Take my life; I am no better than my ancestors." Have you ever felt that the pressures of life were so great that you didn't have the strength to continue? Elijah felt this type of pressure, and the Bible says that God provided him strength for the journey in the form of bread and water. Are you trusting God to provide you with strength for your journey? Or are you trying to do everything on your own? Life can be challenging and though we feel alone, we are never truly alone, because God is always with us. Isaiah 58:11 says, "The

Lord will guide you always; he will satisfy your needs in a sun-scorched land and will strengthen your frame. You will be like a well-watered garden, like a spring whose waters never fail." Because God is for you, it really doesn't matter who is against you. You will be victorious!

Don't Fold Under Pressure

Many people today fold under the ever consuming pressure to live up to the world's standards. The world tells us that we have to look a certain way in order to be considered cool, or we aren't successful unless we make a certain amount of money a year and drive a certain brand name car. The world uses a value system that's based on money and power. What really determines if you are cool by today's standards? In my humble opinion, I believe what should determine if you're cool or not is your relationship with Jesus Christ. After all, what does it profit a man to gain the whole world, and lose his soul? Nothing! Money and power can't keep you from going to hell. The only thing that can do that is accepting Jesus Christ as your Lord and personal savior. Why do we try so hard to live up to the world's standards? The short answer is that we want to belong. We want to be included and not left out. However, if we took the time to seriously think about this, then we would realize that there is no way that we could actually live up to the world's standards. Nothing that you do will ever be good enough according to the world's standards. If you are smart, then they will call you a "know it all". If you have attractive physical features, then you will be considered stuck up or conceited. If you have a small frame or a very large frame, then you are judge based on your size. If you talk about God a lot, then you are considered a "Holy Roller or holier than thou". As followers of Christ, we aren't supposed to cherish the things of this world. 1 John 2:15-17 says, "Do not love the world or anything in the world. If anyone loves the world, love for the Father is not in them. For everything in the world—the lust of the flesh, the lust of the eyes, and the pride of life—comes not from the Father but from the world. The world and its desires pass away, but whoever does the will of God lives forever." God's word tells us that as Christians, we shouldn't be trying to conform to the patterns of this world. Romans 12:2 says, "Do not conform to the pattern of this world, but be transformed by the renewing of your mind. Then you will be able to test and approve what God's will is—his good, pleasing and perfect will." If you are someone who blends into the crowd too easily, or if the unsaved is totally comfortable around you, then you may be dimming your life and compromising your walk with God. Psalm 1:1-2 says, "Blessed is the one who does not walk in step with the wicked or stand in the way that sinners take or sit in the company of mockers, but whose delight is in the law of the Lord, and who meditates on his law day and night." You may be saying to yourself, "Jesus himself spent time around sinners, so why can't I?" It's true that Jesus did spend time around sinners, but he wasn't influenced by them. And they were not his peers (or friends that he was cool with). We should share our faith with those that are unsaved, but their ways shouldn't corrupt us. Our delight should be in the ways of the lord. There are going to be times in life when we have to make a choice. Are you going to choose to live for the world? Or are you going to choose to live for God?

Sometimes we fold under pressure not by what we do, but by what we don't do. Have you ever kept quiet about something that you knew wasn't right? Or have you ever said something about someone that you knew wasn't true? Did you know that when you don't stand up for what you believe, you are folding under pressure? As Christians, we should strive to carry ourselves in such a way that God would be proud of us, not saddened by us. Is God proud of you? Or have you done some things that you know saddened God? If you answered no to these questions, then don't feel bad. We have all sinned and fallen short of the glory of God. The good news is if we repent of our sins, God will forgive us. 1 John 1:9 says, "If we confess our sins, he is faithful and just and will forgive us our sins and purify us from all unrighteousness." If you make choices based on the world's standards, then you will eventually regret your decision. However, if you make choices according to the word of God, then you will never regret your decisions. There's this popular saying that I remember my mother saying a lot when I was growing up and it goes something like this, "If you make your bed hard, then you have to lay in it." What this basically means is, if you put yourself into difficult situations, then you have to deal with the choices that you made, until you can figure out a solution to the problem. When we put ourselves in these situations, we often expect God to rescue us. But sometimes instead of removing us from the situation, he allows us to continue going through it and he protects us while we are in the midst of our various situations. God allows us to go through hardships because he knows that they make us stronger and strengthen our faith. Isaiah 43:2 says, "When you pass through the waters, I will be with you; and when you pass through the rivers, they will not sweep over you. When you walk through the fire, you will not be burned; the flames will not set you ablaze." 1 Peter 1:6-7 says, "In all this you greatly rejoice, though now for a little while you may have had to suffer grief in all kinds of trials. These have come so that the proven genuineness of your faith—of greater worth than gold, which perishes even though refined by fire—may result in praise, glory and honor when Jesus Christ is revealed." If you are going through something and you are wondering why God hasn't changed your circumstances, then there may still be lessons for you to learn.

Sharing the Load

The life of a Christian isn't always easy. We share the same burdens as non-believers, and sometimes more, because of our faith and the example that we are called to be in the world. When we walk with God, the burdens that we carry seem a lot lighter. Often, they don't seem like burdens at all. When we don't walk closely with God, we add the extra weight that comes along with carrying our own burdens. Matthew 11:28-30 says, "Come to me, all you who are weary and burdened, and I will give you rest. Take my yoke upon you and learn from me, for I am gentle and humble in heart, and you will find rest for your souls. For my yoke is easy and my burden is light." Are you carrying extra weight from bearing your own burdens? You may be asking yourself, "What's the difference between burdens and extra weight?" Burdens are the things that have been placed upon us that are beyond our control. These things can be any of the following: growing up in a difficult situation, the loss of a job due to the economy, taking care of a loved one that's sick, or dealing with the responsibilities that a job may place upon you. Extra weights are the things that we place upon ourselves that are within our control. These things can be any of the following: not eating right and taking care of ourselves, doing things that cause problems in our marriage or relationships, making decisions without consulting God and expecting him to bail us out, and committing to things that time doesn't allow us to do. Life can be challenging enough with the burdens that we already carry. But when we add extra weight, we make life that much more difficult.

The Bible says that we are to carry one another's burdens. You may be saying to yourself, "I have enough going on in my own life, how can I carry someone else's burden?" This is actually simpler than you think. Bearing someone else's burden can consist of: taking them to a doctor's appointment, praying for them, or taking them a meal when they can't go and get it themselves. Galatians 6:2-5 says, "Carry each other's burdens, and in this way you will fulfill the law of Christ. If anyone thinks they are something when they are not, they deceive themselves. Each one should test their own actions. Then they can take pride in themselves alone, without comparing themselves to someone else, for each one should carry their own load." While there are many things we can do to help someone bear their burdens, I have discovered that prayer is the most powerful tool that we can use to help others. When bearing the burdens of others, we have to be careful not cripple them in the process. If we are able to offer support to someone while they are going through a crisis, that's a good thing. But you don't want to provide so much support for a person that they become dependent on you for everything. I have seen this many times and the result often leads to the person not being able to do anything for themselves. Can you imagine going through life depending on someone to do everything for you?

While we shouldn't depend on someone to do everything for us, we should learn how to share our burdens with others. I can remember a situation in my own life that happened a few years ago and it required me to learn how to share the load with my significant other. I was accustomed to doing everything on my own. But when I was no longer able to do everything on my own, I had to learn how to share the load with my significant other. When life gets tough, we have to put our pride aside and learn to share the load. 2 Corinthian 8:13-15 says, "Our desire is not that others might be relieved while you are hard pressed, but that there might be equality." At the present time your plenty will supply what they need, so that in turn their plenty will supply what you need. The goal is equality, as it is written: "The one who gathered much did not have too much, and the one who gathered little did not have too little."

Philippians 4:6-7 says, "Do not be anxious about anything, but in every situation, by prayer and petition, with thanksgiving, present your requests to God. And the peace of God, which transcends all understanding, will guard your hearts and your minds in Christ Jesus." Although it may be hard for us to believe sometimes, God understands the pressure that we are faced with each and every day. When life begins to place demands on you and you find yourself exhausted, remember to take some time to rest and pray. During this time, God often reveals to us ways to deal with everything that's being placed upon us. This is also a good time to share your burdens with God and to release some of the things that may be troubling you. Whenever life's burdens become too heavy, remember that you serve a God who is able to handle anything. Nothing is too big or too small for God to handle. Not even the situation or circumstances that you are dealing with right now. If you are willing to share the load, then God is willing to help you bear the load. Deuteronomy 7:9 says, "Know therefore that the Lord your God is God; he is the faithful God, keeping his covenant of love to a thousand generations of those who love him and keep his commandments." What are you waiting on? Try God today! Watch him prove to you that he is faithful.

Overcoming Obstacles

Obstacles can be anything that keeps us from reaching goals, achieving success, or being what God called us to be. Each day comes with its own troubles and difficulties, but every small victory becomes motivation that we can use to increase our faith. When we go through difficult times, we learn who we really are; but most importantly, we learn about God's faithfulness. There are a number of ways to overcome obstacles, but I want to take the time to point out a few that you can put to use in your life right now.

The first thing that we can do is take inventory of our lives. Go before God and ask him to help you see your faults and provide solutions to help you overcome your failures in life. Ask him to show you what he has in store for your future. Many times when we go through things in life, we try to figure everything out on our own, not knowing that we aren't getting anywhere, because we are wondering aimlessly and lack direction.

The second thing that we can do is surrender our will to God. We have so many things that we want to accomplish in life. But the question is, does God want you to pursue and accomplish those things? Does your plan for your life line up with the plans God has for your life? If you aren't sure, then I suggest that you consult with God and find out. The truth is, God's plan for our lives trumps ours every time. If we hadn't aligned ourselves with his will for our lives, then we may waste valuable time that could have been used for something else.

The third thing that we can do is stand on God's promises to increase our faith. During difficult times, our faith is tested repeatedly, and that process often produces faith that's more mature than average. Psalms 119:2 says, "Blessed are those who keep his statutes and seek him with all their heart." The Amplified Bible states, "Blessed (happy, fortunate, to be envied) are they who keep His testimonies, and who seek, inquire for *and* of Him *and* crave Him with the whole heart." None of us have perfect faith, but God's word encourages us to trust him and believe that he is capable of delivering us from our various situations and circumstances.

The fourth thing that we can do is speak positive words over our life. Proverbs 18:21 says, "The tongue has the power of life and death, and those who love it will eat its fruit." Whatever you speak over your life, then that's what it will become. If you believe that you are a failure, then that's what you will become. If you believe that you will never get married, then it will be so. If you believe that you will never make it out of your circumstances, then you won't. If you believe that you won't achieve much success in life, then you won't. Speak encouraging words over your life based on the word of God. Tell yourself that I can do all things through Christ who strengthens me according to Philippians 4:13. When you feel alone say to yourself, "God is with me always, even until the end of the world." When you feel that the things of this world are trying to steal your joy, say to yourself, "Greater is he that is in me, than he that is in the world." Christ is greater than anything that the enemy can throw at you. Trust in him and he will lead you through.

The fifth thing that you can do is stay focused on God. Shift your focus from how big your problems are, to how big your God is. When we spend a lot of time focusing on our problems, they tend to appear bigger than they really are. But when we give them to God, they decrease in size, because nothing can compare to God. Isaiah 40:29 says "He gives strength to the weary and increases the power of the weak." God may not prevent you from enduring your problems, but he will be there to carry you through them.

The sixth thing that we should do is have a solid prayer life. The Bible says that man ought to always pray and not faint. When obstacles in life begin to overwhelm us and they render us helpless, we can take comfort in knowing that the battle can be won through prayer. Many times in life, things will come against us that are beyond our control, but there's no need for us to fear. God is always there to comfort us when we encounter various trials and tribulations. God doesn't allow us to fight our battles alone, because he fights them for us. 2 Chronicles 2:15 says, "He said: "Listen, King Jehoshaphat and all who live in Judah and Jerusalem! This is what the LORD says to you: 'Do not be afraid or discouraged because of this vast army. For the battle is not yours, but God's."

The last and final thing that we can do to overcome obstacles in life is never give up. There's no need for you to quit or give up, because in the end you win. 1 John 5:5 says, "Who is it that overcomes the world? Only the one who believes that Jesus is the Son of God." When we encounter roadblocks in life, we shouldn't be so quick to throw in the towel. Instead, we should trust God wholeheartedly and believe that he is a rewarder of those who diligently seek him. Hebrews 11:6 says, "And without faith it is impossible to please God, because anyone who comes to him must believe that he exists and that he rewards those who earnestly seek him." God understands everything that we go through and he will never allow us to be consumed by our obstacles. He promises us that he will be our guide as we navigate life's journey. Though the journey may be rough, we have to trust him to lead us in all of life's matters.

www.ingramcontent.com/pod-product-compliance
Lightning Source LLC
Chambersburg PA
CBHW050657160426
43194CB00010B/1979